What Do We Know About the Mystery of D. B. Cooper?

by Kirsten Anderson

illustrated by Tim Foley

Penguin Workshop

To the man himself—give me a holler if you're out there, D. B. Cooper—KA

PENGUIN WORKSHOP
An imprint of Penguin Random House LLC, New York

First published in the United States of America by Penguin Workshop,
an imprint of Penguin Random House LLC, New York, 2024

Visit us online at penguinrandomhouse.com.

Library of Congress Cataloging-in-Publication Data is available.

Printed in the United States of America

ISBN 9780593662564 (paperback)   10 9 8 7 6 5 4 3 2 1 WOR
ISBN 9780593662571 (library binding)   10 9 8 7 6 5 4 3 2 1 WOR

Contents

What Do We Know About the Mystery of D. B. Cooper?

It was clear and cool in Vancouver, Washington, on February 10, 1980, and the Ingram family decided to go on a picnic. Dwayne and Patricia Ingram drove with their eight-year-old son, Brian, to Tena Bar, a sandbar on the Columbia River where people often fished for salmon. Dwayne told Brian to clear a patch of sand so he could build a fire. He planned to grill some hot dogs.

Brian swept his arm across the sand like a broom, smoothing it down. As he did so, his arm bumped against something. He brushed away more sand and pulled out a small blackened bundle. He looked at it closely. It was a stack of twenty-dollar bills! Brian kept digging, and pulled out more money. Then he ran to show the stacked bundles to his parents. They counted the money and found a total of $5,800. The family looked to see if there was any more cash in the sand, but didn't find any. Still, $5,800 was a lot of money.

The Ingrams planned to bring it to their bank and get it changed into new bills. But before they did that, they showed their find to a friend, who told them to bring the bills to the US Federal Bureau of Investigation (FBI). The friend believed that the money could be related to a famous unsolved criminal case.

The Ingrams drove to the FBI office in Portland, Oregon, where they met Special Agent Ralph Himmelsbach. He had been working on the case for years and had followed a lot of leads that went nowhere. But he agreed to look at the money Brian had found.

Ralph Himmelsbach

Agent Himmelsbach checked each bill's serial number against a list. (Serial numbers on paper money include the year the bill was printed and a string of other numbers. They can be used to identify a bill.) Slowly, Himmelsbach realized the numbers matched his list! This was some of the money he'd been looking for. It was the first big break in a case that had completely stumped the FBI for almost nine years.

Brian Ingram didn't know it yet, but he had just become part of the story of one of the greatest unsolved crimes in American history. It was a story that had captured the nation's attention in 1971, and still has a hold on people's imaginations today. For decades, people have tried to solve this mystery. Many have dedicated their lives to the investigation. But no one has been able to answer the big question at the center of it all:

Who was D. B. Cooper?

CHAPTER 1
Flying the Friendly—
and Not-so-Friendly—Skies

What is called the "jet age" took off in the United States on October 26, 1958, when a Pan American Airways jet flew from New York City to Paris. The jet-engine aircraft was invented in 1939 and had been used by the military for years, but this was the first civilian flight for American ticket-buying passengers. And it changed travel forever. The best propeller-powered planes once took more than twelve hours to fly from the United States to Europe, but the new jets could get there in only seven. Suddenly, the world felt a lot smaller.

For most people, the new world of jet travel meant a chance to take an exciting vacation.

But for others, it became a way of life. Millionaire business executives, European royalty, and movie stars flew on jets to Paris for some shopping,

to Los Angeles a few days later, and then to Hawaii for a beach vacation. No longer did they have to spend five days on a ship to cross the Atlantic.

Now they could do it in a few hours. Wealthy people who could easily afford to fly became known as "the jet set." The early jet-setters were soon joined by a whole new brand of 1960s celebrities—rock stars, fashion models, and the photographers who captured their extravagant lifestyles on film.

Airlines were anxious to win over their newer, less glamorous customers, too. They tried to make flying as special as possible. Passengers drank champagne served by flight attendants in designer uniforms. Comfortable seats provided more legroom to relax than today's airplanes do. In response, travelers treated flights as if they were going to a fancy restaurant or hotel. Men wore suits and ties. Women wore dresses and gloves.

Style wasn't the only difference between flying then and now. Airplanes and airports had no security. The terminals were set up like large fancy stores. A person could walk up to the counter of a departing flight, buy a ticket with cash, and board the plane. Luggage wasn't screened by an X-ray machine. There weren't any bomb-sniffing dogs in airports.

Why was there no security? Because no one thought anyone boarding a plane planned to do anything but fly. Everyone was much more worried about flight safety while they were in the air than about their fellow passengers committing any crimes.

That all changed on May 1, 1961, when Antulio Ramirez Ortiz held the pilot of a plane bound for Key West, Florida, at knifepoint and demanded that he fly the plane to Cuba. The pilot met Ramirez Ortiz's demand, flew to Cuba, let Ramirez Ortiz off the plane, and

Antulio Ramirez Ortiz

then simply flew back to Florida. When someone illegally takes over any vehicle and forces it to another destination, that's called "hijacking."

Why "Hijacking"?

The origin of the word *hijack* is unclear. Some people believe that it came from a combination of "highwayman," the centuries-old British term for thieves who robbed travelers along roads, and "jack," which can be used to mean "hold up." Another story says that it came from miners in Missouri in the 1800s, who called the zinc ore they mined "jack." Miners occasionally slipped some of the "high jack," or top-quality zinc, into their boots or pockets in order to sell the valuable mineral for extra cash. "High jack" showed up again in the Prohibition-era of the 1920s, when selling alcoholic beverages was illegal, and powerful gangs fought over the business of getting alcohol into the nightclubs and bars that wanted it. "Hijackers" held up the gangs' trucks as they made deliveries, and stole the illegal alcohol for their own profit. By the mid-twentieth century, it had taken on the meaning people know today: to steal a vehicle (or the goods it carries) directly from its driver (or pilot!).

When someone takes over a plane, it is often called "skyjacking." This was the first successful hijacking of an American airplane. But it would not be the last.

Several more airplane hijackings took place in 1961. At the time, there were no charges to cover this specific crime! Someone could be charged simply with transporting a stolen airplane across state lines. By 1968, they were happening at an alarming pace. Like Ramirez Ortiz, many hijackers wanted to go to Cuba, a small island nation off the coast of Florida.

Some had lost faith in the American way of life. They thought that Cuba, governed by the dictator Fidel Castro, was a country where everyone was treated equally. Hijackers felt that Castro would welcome them like heroes

Fidel Castro

for turning away from their lives in the United States.

They were wrong. The people of communist Cuba had very little freedom or opportunities. Castro did not consider the hijackers to be heroes. Instead, he put them in jail or into work camps. And the United States had to pay him for the return of the airplanes.

The US Senate met to discuss the hijacking problem. One senator suggested that the airlines put metal detectors in airports to catch people carrying guns or knives. The airlines said no. They thought that would scare passengers. Some travelers might get impatient or annoyed about the invasion of their privacy. Also, the airlines just didn't want to spend money on security equipment. The airlines decided that they couldn't stop hijackers. Instead, they focused on making sure no lives were lost. They told flight crews to do whatever hijackers asked of them. They gave their pilots maps of Cuba and lists of useful Spanish phrases.

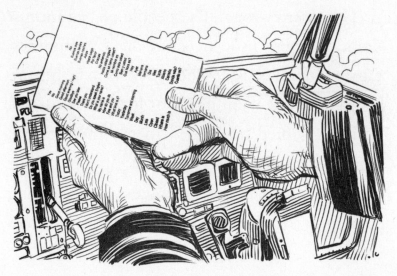

In the first six weeks of 1969, there were eleven skyjackings in the United States. This was a new type of crime wave that began to happen once a week, or sometimes twice in one day!

Not all of the skyjackers wanted to go to Cuba, though. When they discovered that airplane crews would do little to stop them, they demanded money instead. Most of them failed in their requests for large sums of cash. They made mistakes and were captured, or ended up surrendering.

Except for one.

CHAPTER 2
The Man in 18E

November 24, 1971, began as usual for Northwest Orient Airlines Flight 305. The Boeing 727 took off from Washington, DC, then

made stops across the Upper Midwest and then in Spokane, Washington. Portland International Airport was the second to last stop on the route before the plane would end its journey in Washington State at Seattle-Tacoma Airport, known as SEA-TAC.

A freezing cold wind blew into the plane from the open door at the top of the stairs in Portland,

Flo Schaffner

where twenty-three-year-old flight attendant
Flo Schaffner waited for the new passengers.
Schaffner had joined the flight in Minnesota.
It was Wednesday, the day before Thanksgiving,
and she couldn't wait to go see her family in
Arkansas the next day.

Flo Schaffner greeted each passenger.

"Welcome aboard. Can I check your ticket?"

The passengers handed Schaffner their tickets, then headed into the plane's cabin. Most were on their way home for Thanksgiving.

"Hi. Welcome aboard."

The passenger wore a black suit and tie and a black raincoat. He also carried a briefcase.

Businessman, Schaffner thought. She looked at the name on the ticket. It said *Dan Cooper*.

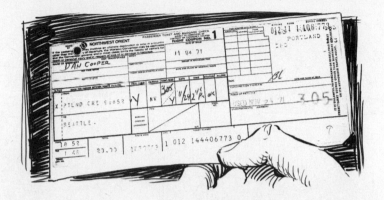

A few minutes later, Schaffner shut the door. There weren't many passengers. The plane was less than half full.

It was a short flight from Portland to Seattle, only about a half hour long. Schaffner started taking the passengers' drink orders immediately, before the plane even took off. The man in the black suit sat in the last row of the plane, seat 18E, on the right side next to the window. His briefcase was on the seat next to him. He ordered a bourbon and soda and gave Schaffner a twenty-dollar bill. The drink only cost a dollar, though. Schaffner told him she would come back later with change.

Soon it was time for takeoff. Alice Hancock, the first-class flight attendant, went to her seat near the front door of the plane. Schaffner and Tina Mucklow, another flight attendant, headed to the back to take their seats by the airplane's rear door.

Tina Mucklow

Alice Hancock

"Miss?"

Schaffner looked up. It was the man from seat 18E. He handed her an envelope. She dropped it in her purse without even looking at it. Schaffner was pretty sure she knew what it was: Another traveler giving her his phone number, hoping for a date. This type of flirting seemed to happen all the time.

The plane sped down the runway, about to tip its nose up and lift into the sky.

"Miss?"

It was that man again. "I think you better have a look at that note."

Schaffner reached into her purse for the envelope. She opened it and took out the note. She read the neatly written words:

Miss,

I have a bomb here and I would like you to sit by me.

CHAPTER 3
Hijacked

"You're kidding, right?" Flo Schaffner asked.

She had moved into the seat next to the man in the black suit, just as he had requested.

"No, miss," he replied.

He opened his briefcase. Inside were eight red sticks, about six inches long. Were they dynamite?

Schaffner wasn't sure if it was a real bomb, but she knew she couldn't take any chances. Terrified, she turned back to Tina Mucklow, and tried to call her name, but no words came out.

Tina Mucklow saw that Schaffner seemed upset about something. Then she noticed the note lying on the floor, where Schaffner had dropped it when she changed seats. Mucklow picked up and read the note. She was only twenty-two years old, the youngest and lowest-ranked member of the flight crew, but she knew what to do. Mucklow went to the phone at the  rear of the plane and called the cockpit.

"We're being hijacked. He's got a bomb and this is no joke."

Captain William Scott, whom everyone called

Captain William Scott

Scotty, was the pilot. He was in the cockpit with the copilot, Bill Rataczak, and the flight engineer, Harold Anderson. Scotty had been a pilot during World War II, flying missions through the Himalayan mountain range that extends along Northern India's border with China. He knew how to stay calm in difficult situations. Scotty immediately got on his radio to contact Northwest Orient's headquarters in Minneapolis and let them know that Flight 305 had a man with a bomb on board.

Back in the eighteenth row, the hijacker put on sunglasses and told Schaffner to write down his demands. He said he wanted $200,000 in cash, delivered in a knapsack at the Seattle airport by 5:00 p.m. He also wanted two front parachutes and two back parachutes. A fuel truck should be waiting for them, ready to start refueling the plane immediately. The hijacker also asked for meals for the flight crew to be sent along with everything else. He made it clear that he would set off the bomb if anyone tried to stop him. He intended to collect the money and parachutes in Seattle, and then have the plane take off again with plenty of fuel.

Schaffner tried to stay calm as she wrote it all down, but she was very nervous. She got up to bring the note to the cockpit, but then the hijacker said she had to stay with him. Mucklow offered to deliver it, but the hijacker said no. Finally, he said Schaffner could bring the note to the cockpit and told Mucklow to sit by him.

They agreed and Mucklow took the seat next to the hijacker. When he showed her the bomb in his briefcase, she felt so scared that she almost threw up. However, she knew she had to remain calm so she wouldn't upset the other passengers— or the hijacker.

The plane was still rising, its nose pointed upward, forcing Schaffner to walk slightly uphill as she made her way to the cockpit. Once she

was safely inside, she gave the list of demands to Scotty, who radioed the airline again and told them what the hijacker wanted.

Back in the cabin, Mucklow tried to make some conversation with the hijacker. He asked where she was from, and she told him she had grown up in Pennsylvania, but that she lived in Minnesota now. Tina Mucklow was trying to remain calm, but she was very afraid. She wanted to run. But there was nowhere to run.

Meanwhile, back in Minneapolis, Northwest Orient's executives told the crew of Flight 305 and the Seattle airport to do anything the hijacker wanted. They didn't want to risk anyone being hurt or having one of their planes blown up by a hijacker.

That set off a frantic scramble to meet the hijacker's demands. A detective from the Seattle police department raced to Seattle First National Bank, where employees were waiting with $200,000 in cash. The bank handed over a sack filled with one hundred bundles, each holding a hundred twenty-dollar bills. All the bills had been photographed so the bank would have a list of their serial numbers.

Washington state troopers were on their way to SEA-TAC with one set of parachutes that they had picked up from a nearby skydiving school. A local pilot had supplied the other set, which was already at the airport.

FBI agents had also rushed to SEA-TAC to be ready to meet the plane. Other agents went to Portland to question people there who might have seen the hijacker when he boarded the flight.

Scotty called Tina Mucklow on the in-plane phone and asked if they should tell the passengers why they weren't preparing to land. The hijacker said no, and told Scotty to make something up. The pilot announced that the plane was having a minor mechanical issue and they would have to circle SEA-TAC for a while.

A passenger wandered toward the back of the plane, but Mucklow stopped him and asked what he wanted. He said he was just looking for a magazine. Mucklow found one and sent him back to his seat. Another passenger came back to complain about the landing being delayed. As he got angrier, the hijacker told him to stop bothering the flight attendant and go back to his seat.

Tina Mucklow tried to make conversation by asking the man in seat 18E where he was from, but of course he wouldn't tell her. Then she asked why he chose to hijack this flight. He said, "I don't have a grudge against your airline, miss.

I just have a grudge." (A grudge is resentment or anger toward something or someone.) Flight 305 just happened to be the right plane at the right place and the right time for him to act on his grudge.

It was raining hard as the plane circled the airport. The hijacker complained to Mucklow that he had expected to have the money by 5:00 and it was already 5:15. Mucklow called Scotty to ask about the delay. He told her that they were waiting for the parachutes to arrive before he would land the plane. Scotty believed they were being brought over from McChord Air Force Base near Seattle. The hijacker then said that the base was only twenty minutes from Tacoma. It shouldn't take this long.

Scotty called again and said that the parachutes were almost at the airport. He asked the hijacker if he could begin the landing process. This time the hijacker said yes.

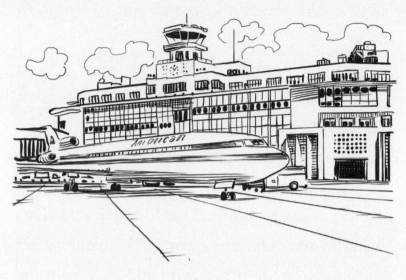

SEA-TAC

SEA-TAC had been completely closed down. Other incoming flights were told to circle the airport or were sent to different locations. The FBI was on the scene. Officials in Washington, DC, listened in on the radio communications. The pilots on a flight that had been grounded at SEA-TAC played the radio conversations between Scotty and FBI agents on speakers so the passengers could keep up as the drama unfolded.

News trucks waited near the airport to report on the story.

Flight 305 finally landed at SEA-TAC at 5:45 p.m., almost three hours after it had left Portland. The runway was lit by huge lights, the kind used on movie sets. A truck drove up to the plane and began to pump fuel into it. An FBI car waited nearby. The hijacker sent Tina Mucklow out the front door of the plane to get the money. She returned with the sack from the bank. It was heavy, more than twenty pounds. Then she asked if the passengers could leave. The man said yes.

The weary passengers made their way down the stairs into the wet, dark night, then boarded a bus to bring them to the airport terminal. Most of them didn't know they had been hijacked until an FBI agent boarded the bus. They hadn't noticed what had been going on in the back of the plane.

The agent began to read from a list of passenger names. Each person responded as their name was called.

"Dan Cooper?"

There was no response.

"Dan Cooper?"

CHAPTER 4
Jump

Alice Hancock and Flo Schaffner carefully approached the hijacker. They asked if they could get their purses from the seats behind him.

"Sure," he said. "I'm not going to bite you." The hijacker told Schaffner and Hancock they could leave the airplane, then he asked Mucklow to pull down the shades on each window. When she got back to him, she looked around the cabin. It was empty, except for her and the hijacker. Although the pilots were still in the cockpit, she felt very alone.

The hijacker now seemed angry. He had asked for the money to come in a knapsack he could wear and this was just an open-top canvas sack without any strings, zippers, or handles. How could he jump while holding it, without the money falling out? He opened one of the front parachutes, then cut the cords that connected the parachute canopy to the pack. He used those to tie up the top of the sack.

The crew got a call from Mucklow, with new instructions from the hijacker. They should fly to Mexico City, staying at an altitude of 10,000 feet. That's a much lower altitude than usual for jets. He wanted the plane to fly at a slow speed, with the rear door open and back stairs down.

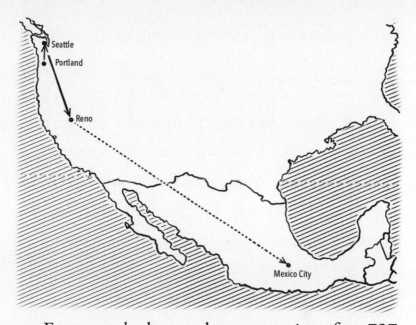

Few people knew the rear stairs of a 727 plane could be let down after takeoff. Most other planes didn't even have rear stairs. The hijacker also knew that at 10,000 feet, the airplane cabin wouldn't be pressurized. When flying at high altitudes, where the air is thin and hard to breathe, airplane cabins are pressurized so the passengers can breathe normally. But if a door is opened while the cabin is pressurized, a person can be sucked out the open door. At 10,000 feet, the hijacker could safely open a door. In addition to knowing the Washington State area, he seemed to know a lot about planes and flying.

The crew called Mucklow and told her that they couldn't take off with the stairs down, but that they could open them once they were in the air. She explained this to the hijacker, and he agreed to take off with them up. The crew also said that flying slowly at that altitude burned extra fuel. They would need to refuel again on the way to Mexico. The crew suggested that they stop at the airport in Yuma, Arizona, or Reno, Nevada. The hijacker chose Reno.

The crew waited to get a flight plan from Northwest Orient. They were required to file an official plan with all the details about the flight to Mexico City with a stop in Reno before the airport could clear them for takeoff. But the hijacker was getting impatient. He picked up the phone and yelled into it.

"Let's get this show on the road!"

Mucklow asked if she could go up to the cockpit with the crew. She didn't understand why he wanted her back there in the cabin with him. The hijacker said he needed her to lower the stairs once they were in the air.

That scared Mucklow. She feared that she might get sucked out of the plane when the door opened. She didn't know she would be safe at 10,000 feet. Then the hijacker changed his mind. He said she could just show him how to put down the stairs and then go into the cockpit. Mucklow demonstrated how to work the stairs. It was easy—he just had to pull one lever.

The hijacker asked her to turn off the lights in the cabin so the only light left was the reading light over his seat. He complained again about how long it was taking. The crew said they were still waiting to file the flight plan and the hijacker told them to take off without it. The pilots could send in the plan over the radio while in flight.

As the plane began to taxi down the runway, Mucklow and the hijacker took seats in row 18. A few minutes after takeoff, the hijacker told Mucklow to pull the curtain that separated the first-class section from the main cabin closed, then go into the cockpit and stay there with the crew.

Before leaving, Mucklow asked about the bomb. The man in the black suit said he'd either take it with him or disable it. The last thing Mucklow saw as she moved toward the front of the plane was the hijacker tying the sack of money around his waist. When she entered the cockpit, she felt a tremendous sense of relief. The crew wasn't safe yet, but at least she was no longer with the hijacker.

As Flight 305 finally took off again, fighter
jets from the nearby air force base took off, too.
They tried to stay as close to Flight 305 as they
could without being seen. Other military aircraft
joined them as the plane headed toward Nevada.

They were tailing the plane to watch out for signs of danger. What if the hijacker became desperate and tried to crash the plane into a city? They were prepared to shoot it down.

The hijacker called the cockpit to say he was  having trouble with the stairs. Then a light on the cockpit dashboard signaled to the crew that the stairs were, in fact, down. Still, copilot Bill Rataczak called back to the cabin. When the hijacker answered, Rataczak could hear hurricane-force winds blowing in the cabin, a sign that the door was open. He asked if there was anything they could help him with. The hijacker said no.

Bill Rataczak

The thermometer outside the plane said it was seven degrees below zero Fahrenheit. With wind shooting in from the open door, it must have been freezing in the cabin. Rataczak called again and asked if everything was okay. The hijacker said yes.

The crew watched their dashboard. Suddenly, the instruments showed a change in air pressure in the cabin. It was a little past 8:00 p.m. They called the hijacker. No one answered.

When the plane got close to Reno, Mucklow called back again. She said that the stairs needed to be put up before they landed, or the plane might be damaged. Again, there was no response. The stairs dangling from the back of the plane made a shrieking noise as the plane touched down in Reno and raced down the runway. When it finally came to a stop, Scotty unlocked the cockpit door, then he and Mucklow carefully walked through first class. They opened the curtain and looked back into the main cabin. It was empty.

The man in the dark suit was gone.

CHAPTER 5
The Search Begins

The flight crew searched the cabin thoroughly. They even crawled down the aisle, looking under the seats. Mucklow was still nervous about the bomb and wanted to make sure it was gone. They didn't find anything—or anyone. Finally, the crew was able to exit the plane. When they got into the FBI car to take them to the terminal, Mucklow broke down and cried. It was over.

The FBI swarmed the cabin of the plane, looking for evidence. They dusted for fingerprints by coating surfaces with a special powder. They picked up the butts from the cigarettes the hijacker had smoked and pulled the plastic cup he drank from out of the trash. They found a few hairs and the man's tie. It was a narrow black clip-on tie, nothing fancy. He had also left two parachutes. One was the front parachute that he had cut up and used to tie the open-top sack of money to his waist. The other was one of the back parachutes. All of it was now evidence.

While the hijacking was still in progress, the story had become national news. When an FBI agent spoke to reporters at the Portland airport, he told them that the hijacker bought a ticket under the name "D. Cooper." But one of the reporters heard it wrong and wrote down

"D. B. Cooper." When that reporter's story was printed in newspapers around the world, the hijacker became known as D. B. Cooper, even though the original name on his ticket had been "Dan Cooper."

The next night, Walter Cronkite, the famous TV newsman, spoke about the hijacking. He called Cooper a "master criminal."

Walter Cronkite

For the FBI, the hijacking *was* a criminal case. "Air piracy," as it was known, was a serious crime. The hijacker could be sentenced to decades in prison. In some places, skyjackers could be sentenced to death. Cooper had threatened to blow up an airplane with a bomb. People could have been killed.

For some Americans, though, D. B. Cooper didn't seem like a criminal. In the early 1970s, many people were unemployed, while prices kept going up. People were angry at big businesses. They thought the hijacker was a hero. After all, no one had been hurt. Cooper had gotten money from an airline, a huge multimillion-dollar business. They applauded him for "sticking it to the man," which means taking action to defy authority. It seemed like Cooper had committed the perfect crime.

A TV news reporter asked a man on the street if he thought Cooper was a hero. The man said, "Oh, sure. . . . 'Cause the guy, evidently, really took a lot of time to plan the whole thing out. And I respect a man who takes his time to do a job well done."

Parachutes: Safety First!

Since the early days of skydiving, jumpers have almost always worn two parachutes. The back parachute is the main parachute and the front parachute is a reserve or backup. The reserve parachute is there in case the main parachute fails to open.

Today's parachutes have many kinds of safety features. Reserve parachutes have a device that measures the skydiver's rate of descent and their altitude. If the skydiver falls to a certain altitude at a high speed, that tells the device that the main parachute hasn't opened. Then the reserve will open automatically. Modern parachutes also have one handle that can cut away a malfunctioning main parachute and another to manually open the reserve.

For extra safety, beginning skydivers don't

even have to jump alone. In a tandem jump, a new jumper is attached to an instructor. The instructor makes sure that everything works correctly, and the first-timer can just enjoy the ride.

CHAPTER 6
NORJAK

It was too dark and rainy on the night of the hijacking to begin a search on the ground immediately. So the FBI didn't really begin until almost two days later, on November 26. They put together a guess about where Cooper had jumped based on the moment in the flight when the pilots had noticed the change in air pressure.

They thought the change was from Cooper jumping off the stairs, causing them to bounce. The search area, called the "drop zone," was about twenty-five square miles in southwest Washington State, near Lake Merwin and a town called Ariel.

Police officers and sheriff's deputies from the surrounding counties combed through the densely forested search area. The trees there are tall and the ground is covered in thick layers of brambles.

It was hard for anyone to walk, let alone search for evidence. Helicopters and airplanes buzzed overhead, looking for broken branches, a tangled parachute caught in a treetop, or smoke from a campfire. FBI agents went door-to-door in nearby towns, asking if anyone had seen or heard anything strange on the night of the hijacking.

Soon the searchers got some unexpected help. Civilians from around the Pacific Northwest joined the search, but not because they were all interested in finding D. B. Cooper. Some were hoping to find the $200,000 he had carried with him when he jumped from the plane! Meanwhile, Northwest Orient offered a $25,000 reward to anyone who found the money. A Seattle newspaper offered $5,000 for information that led to the capture of Cooper.

The FBI had interviewed Flight 305's passengers and crew immediately after the hijacking. Then they interviewed them several more times over the next few days. Almost everyone agreed that the hijacker was in his mid-forties, about six feet tall, maybe around 170 pounds. Most witnesses said his skin was somewhat tan, and that he had short dark hair. Flo Schaffner, the only person who saw him without his sunglasses, said his eyes were brown.

The people who spoke with him said he didn't have an accent that stood out. Just about everyone agreed that he wore a black suit, white shirt, black tie, and black raincoat with brown shoes. Many of the passengers had barely noticed him. They said they wouldn't recognize him if they saw him again.

Tina Mucklow had spent the most time with Cooper. She said he seemed like an executive, an important businessman. Mucklow said that Cooper didn't seem nervous and he never tried to hurt her. He was impatient at times, but he was never "cruel or nasty . . . or impolite" to her.

The FBI produced a few sketches of Cooper based on these descriptions and released them to the public. They also sent a list of the ransom money's serial numbers to FBI offices around the country, as well as to businesses including motels and restaurants. Eventually, they let newspapers publish the list so anyone could check whether they had found any of the stolen twenty-dollar bills.

D. B. Cooper

The FBI named the case NORJAK, which was short for Northwest Airliner Hijacking, and began to put together a profile of the hijacker. Guessing at first that only an expert parachutist would have attempted such a dangerous jump, FBI agents  investigated skydivers and parachuting schools all over the Pacific Coast. Cooper had known a lot about the plane, so they also interviewed engineers and test pilots who had worked at the Boeing factory in Everett, Washington. But everyone they spoke to either didn't fit the description, or had a reason why they couldn't have been on Flight 305 that night.

Strangely, newspapers and FBI offices received many letters from people insisting they *were* Cooper. Most seemed to be pranks or didn't fit the facts of the case. They were dismissed as fakes.

Others made money off the Cooper mystery. They sold D. B. Cooper T-shirts. A singer named Judy Sword wrote a song about him called, "D. B. Cooper, Where Are You?"

That was the question everyone was asking.

CHAPTER 7
Citizen Detectives

The search on the ground continued through December. FBI agents and police covered over eight hundred square miles without finding anything. Wintry weather made it impossible to trek through the forest where Cooper may have landed. But the search picked up again in the spring when the army sent soldiers and helicopters to look for Cooper. The soldiers camped in the area for weeks and searched every day.

Ralph Himmelsbach, one of the FBI agents investigating the NORJAK case, wasn't surprised that no one had caught Cooper. He was sure the hijacker hadn't survived the jump. It had been a freezing, rainy night and the man had jumped out of a plane into a forest wearing a business suit and dress shoes. How could anyone survive that? Many others at the FBI agreed with Himmelsbach.

They thought they were more likely to find a body, a parachute, or just the money, rather than Cooper alive and well.

Still, Himmelsbach and other agents investigated every lead the FBI received. Once the sketch of Cooper was released, tips from the public poured into FBI offices. People called or sent letters to report all kinds of possible suspects. A man in the crowd at a football game looked like the Cooper sketch. A former high school classmate fit the description. A server at a restaurant was given an unusually large tip by a customer. Could it have been Cooper, spending his ransom money?

Months turned into years. By 1975, the FBI had investigated eight hundred leads. There weren't any new clues or evidence. Anyone considered a suspect had been cleared.

Seven years later, in November 1978, a hunter found a plastic card in the area of the drop zone that explained how to open the rear stairs on a Boeing 727.

EMERGENCY
EXIT HANDLE
AFT AIRSTAIR
TO OPERATE
OPEN ACCESS DOOR, PULL ON RED HANDLE. LOCK WIRE WILL BREAK WHEN HANDLE IS PULLED

The FBI determined that it had fallen from Flight 305. But it didn't lead to any new information. The agency was no closer to solving the NORJAK case than they were the moment Cooper jumped from the plane.

The only real break in the case came in 1980 when eight-year-old Brian Ingram found $5,800 buried in the sand along the Columbia River. That discovery set off a massive new search. People dug through sand along the river, hoping to find more money, but no money or any other clues were found. Actually, it only made things more confusing. How did some of the money end up so many miles away from the FBI's drop zone? Some people began to wonder

Brian Ingram

if the FBI had spent almost a decade looking in the wrong place.

In 2007, FBI agent Larry Carr took over the NORJAK case. By that time, the FBI was reluctant to put more time or money into searching for Cooper. So Carr did what everyone in the twenty-first century does to

Larry Carr

get information—he went online. Carr joined a message board devoted to finding Cooper. He shared information to help the community with their research. In 2009, Carr let a team of citizen detectives who met online analyze evidence from the case. The group, mostly made up of scientists, studied the money found by Brian Ingram. They tested how bundles of bills move in water and came to believe that the money had not floated down the river, as many people had suggested. They believed it was buried there by someone.

But who buried the money? Was it Cooper? Or someone else?

In 2016, the FBI officially closed the D. B. Cooper case. The agency said it wanted to put its time and resources into more current cases. Soon after, a group of amateur investigators sued to have the FBI release its NORJAK case files. They won, and now the FBI's entire vault of

D. B. Cooper information is available online.

The team of scientists continued to study the evidence. In 2017, new analysis of the tie showed the presence of pure titanium. Titanium is a chemical element that can be made into a thin, strong metal. In the early 1970s, very few products were made out of pure titanium. The team thinks this means Cooper may have worked for one of the rare companies that used it, most likely a certain type of chemical plant or metal manufacturer. In 2020, they found particles on the money that suggested that it had been buried in the spring, several months after the hijacking.

They also noted that in the 1970s, only a manager or engineer would have worn a tie at a factory. Cooper wore a suit and tie. Maybe Cooper was an engineer or manager for a metal or chemical company who lost his job and hoped to get revenge. Maybe that was the "grudge" he mentioned to Tina Mucklow.

Albert Weinberg

The online Cooper community came across another interesting clue. In the 1960s, a Belgian comic book artist created a comic book series about a Royal Canadian Air Force combat pilot who was named Dan Cooper.

The artist, Albert Weinberg, had often drawn pictures of pilot Dan Cooper parachuting out of airplanes. Maybe the hijacker had used the name of a favorite comic book character  when he bought the ticket for Flight 305. But the Cooper comics were written in French. They never were translated into English and were not well-known in the United States.

The flight attendants who spoke with Cooper said he didn't have a foreign accent. Could he have been a member of the US military who served in Europe and found the comics there? Or a Canadian who spoke both English and French? Should people have been looking for an angry skydiving unemployed Canadian engineer?

Perhaps one who suddenly had a lot of money in 1971? Maybe! Or maybe not.

These are just a few of the theories people have come up with about the Cooper hijacking. There are many, many more.

CHAPTER 8
Suspects

Over the years, the FBI dismissed every suspect they investigated due to lack of evidence, or because the suspect didn't match the physical description given by witnesses. Other people continue to consider possible suspects. Some of them are sure they have found D. B. Cooper.

Robert Rackstraw is one of the best-known Cooper suspects. Amateur investigators have written books and appeared in documentaries trying to prove that Rackstraw was Cooper. Rackstraw served as a paratrooper during the Vietnam War and also was a helicopter pilot. After Rackstraw was dismissed from the army for misconduct, he was arrested for writing bad checks, domestic violence, and even was charged

**RACKSTRAW
ROBERT W**

Robert Rackstraw

with the murder of his stepfather. A jury found him not guilty and he later faked his own death to escape charges of carrying illegal explosives.

For some Cooper investigators, Rackstraw's military experience and criminal record make him the ideal suspect. They also believe he looked like the FBI's sketches. He even sometimes hinted to people that he just might be D. B. Cooper.

The FBI didn't find any evidence to show that Rackstraw was Cooper. Also, he was only twenty-eight at the time of the hijacking, around twenty years younger than the hijacker was. Still, many people believe Rackstraw was D. B. Cooper.

Richard Floyd McCoy Jr. is another popular suspect. A few months after the Cooper hijacking, McCoy hijacked an airplane using almost the

Richard Floyd McCoy Jr.

exact same plan as Cooper. He had a gun and a hand grenade, asked for the same type of parachutes, and demanded $500,000. He jumped out of the plane over Utah, where he lived, and went home. A few days later, McCoy was arrested. McCoy was sent to prison for the hijacking in 1972, but escaped two years later—and was killed in a shootout with law enforcement.

Agent Himmelsbach had investigated McCoy, whom he said was too short and had the wrong color eyes to be Cooper. In 2007, Larry Carr had DNA from McCoy's family tested against DNA samples from Cooper's tie. DNA is the code found in the human body that gives people their hair color, eye color, and other unique qualities. No two people have the same DNA. The FBI's test results showed that McCoy wasn't Cooper. But the FBI lab also warned that the DNA sample from the tie was weak and couldn't really prove or disprove anything. Still, some people insist that McCoy was Cooper.

When Duane Weber was dying in 1995, he told his wife, Jo, that he was "Dan Cooper." At first she didn't know what he meant. Then friends told her about the D. B. Cooper hijacking, and Jo began to investigate. Jo discovered that before she met him, Duane lived his life as a criminal under the name John Collins.

Duane Weber

Duane also had a limp that he claimed came from a long-ago airplane crash, and Jo thought he looked like the FBI sketch of Cooper. But others disagree. A passenger who sat near Cooper during the flight said that Weber's ears stuck out too much for him to be Cooper.

Kenneth Christiansen was a longtime flight attendant for Northwest Orient Airlines and a former army paratrooper. In the 1990s, he told his brother Lyle that he had something important

to confess, but the family stopped him before he could say anything. After seeing a TV program about Cooper, Lyle decided that his brother looked a lot like the Cooper sketches. He was an experienced parachutist

Kenneth Christiansen

and he was very familiar with Boeing 727s. But the FBI had dismissed Christiansen as a suspect because he was too short.

Marla Cooper was an eight-year-old girl growing up in Oregon when the hijacking took place. She remembered that around Thanksgiving in 1971, her favorite uncle, named Lynn Doyle "L. D." Cooper, seemed to be planning something mysterious with another of her uncles. On Thanksgiving morning, she said her uncles drove up to her house and Uncle L. D.

Marla Cooper

had blood on his shirt. They told her he'd been hurt in an automobile accident. Later, she said, she heard one of her uncles say, "Well, we did it. We hijacked an airplane. We're rich. Our money problems are over." L. D. left Oregon about a year later and Marla never saw him again. Years afterward, Marla told the FBI about her uncle, but the only thing connecting him to the hijacking is her memories. There is no actual evidence.

Many other people have confessed to family or friends that they were Cooper. While there usually isn't any evidence that they were the hijacker, there also isn't any evidence that they *weren't*. It seems as if anyone could have been D. B. Cooper.

CHAPTER 9
Where Are You, D. B. Cooper?

Between 1968 and 1972, more than 130 US flights were hijacked. In November 1972, three men hijacked a plane and threatened to crash it into a nuclear power plant if they did not get ten million dollars. A crash like that could release deadly radiation into the air, endangering everyone in the area. The airline

paid the hijackers what they could on such short notice— more than two million dollars. The hijackers then forced the pilots to fly them to Cuba—where the three new millionaires were imprisoned.

The fear that some hijackers might use a plane as a weapon finally convinced the government and airlines to act. By 1974, every airport had to have metal detectors and X-ray machines to screen carry-on bags. After the 9/11 terrorist attacks and other hijacking attempts in the early 2000s, airport security became even stricter with new regulations.

The Ingram family sued the FBI to get back the $5,800 in Cooper money found by Brian in 1980. After a long legal battle, a court decided in 1986 that the Ingrams had to split the money with Northwest Orient Airlines' insurance company. The FBI was allowed to keep fourteen bills as evidence. In 2008, Brian auctioned off several of his blackened, torn bills for about $37,000. People were willing to pay a lot of money to own a piece of history from the D. B. Cooper mystery.

Brian Ingram, 2008

D. B. Cooper has become part of pop culture. There have been several songs written about him, as well as books, movies, and documentaries.

One episode of the Marvel TV series *Loki* suggested that Loki, the mischievous Norse god, might in fact be D. B. Cooper!

Why are people still so fascinated by D. B. Cooper? For some, it's because he's the guy who committed "the perfect crime." They love the idea that he seemed to get away with the skyjacking while not hurting anyone. For others, it's just the lure of the mystery. Every day, people log on to Cooper message boards and visit the FBI vault of Cooper evidence, hoping they'll find some new clues or suspects. Some have devoted their lives to finding Cooper. They dream of being the one who cracks the case that even the FBI couldn't solve.

The 9/11 Attacks Change Airport Security

On September 11, 2001, almost three thousand people were killed when terrorists hijacked four passenger airplanes in a planned attack. The hijackers crashed one plane into the Pentagon, the headquarters of the US Department of Defense, and another went down in a field in Pennsylvania. The other two planes flew into the World Trade Center, two very tall office buildings in New York City, causing them to collapse. After 9/11, airport security changed. The Transportation Security Administration (TSA) was created to increase security for travelers. Cockpit doors in airplanes were reinforced to keep terrorists from reaching the pilots. All baggage had to be screened for dangerous materials by X-ray machines. Passengers had to present ID, take off their shoes, and go through full body scanners to see if they were carrying weapons. Small bottles of liquids that could contain explosive materials were also banned from airplanes.

Investigating the NORJAK case might be a fun hobby for some people, but it wasn't fun for those who were part of it. Flo Schaffner lived in fear for years, worried that Cooper might find her and kill her so she wouldn't identify him. People have called Tina Mucklow for decades, hoping she will confirm that their theories are correct or give them more information. She has been the subject of strange rumors, and had her memory called into question. She has said everything she has to say. The D. B. Cooper case is still the only unsolved hijacking in American history. And there's a good reason why it hasn't been solved—because it's a difficult puzzle! Every idea or piece of evidence can be seen in different ways. Every question has many different answers. Some people say only an expert parachutist would attempt such a dangerous jump. Others think that only an inexperienced skydiver would make the mistake of jumping out of an airplane on a dark, cold, rainy night while wearing a business suit. Still others believe an expert would know better than to even try it. Was Cooper a master criminal with a long record of crimes? Someone with the experience to pull off a big heist? Or was he a desperate man with nothing to lose? When people look at the police sketch and description of the hijacker, they can see anyone they want to believe is Cooper. He was a very ordinary-looking man.

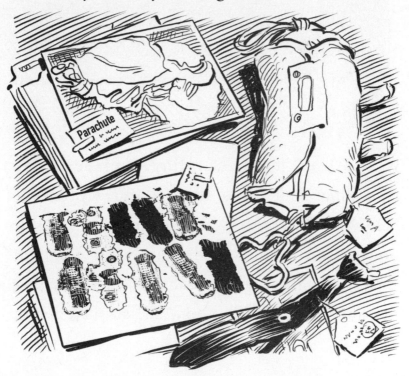

It's been more than fifty years since the hijacking. And here's all anyone really knows: On November 24, 1971, a man in a black suit and raincoat who called himself Dan Cooper boarded a flight from Portland to Seattle. He said he wanted $200,000 or he would set off a bomb.

He got his money and the passengers got off the plane safely. Then, somewhere between Seattle, Washington, and Reno, Nevada, he opened the back door of the airplane, stepped out into the night sky, and vanished.

Timeline of the Mystery of D. B. Cooper

1961 — The first successful hijacking of a US passenger plane takes place

1971 — A man calling himself Dan Cooper hijacks Northwest Orient Flight 305 on November 24

— The search for Cooper begins on November 26

— Police and FBI agents search more than eight hundred square miles of the drop zone beginning in December

1978 — A hunter finds a card explaining how to open Flight 305's rear stairs

1980 — Brian Ingram finds $5,800 of the Cooper ransom money buried on a beach along the Columbia River

1986 — A court decides that the Ingram family can split the Cooper money with Northwest Orient Airlines' insurance company

2009 — The FBI allows a team of private citizens who are interested in the case to analyze the Cooper money and his black necktie

2016 — The FBI officially closes the NORJAK case, but another group of citizen detectives successfully sues to have the case files opened to the public

2017 — Flakes of pure titanium are found on Cooper's tie

2020 — New analysis of the Cooper money gives evidence that it was buried in the spring after the hijacking

Timeline of the World

1961 —	Construction begins on the Berlin Wall, which would cut off communist East Berlin from democratic West Berlin for the next thirty years
1969 —	Astronaut Neil Armstrong becomes the first person to walk on the moon
1972 —	Atari's *Pong*, created by Nolan Bushnell and Allan Alcorn, is released as an arcade game
1977 —	The first *Star Wars* movie, now called *Star Wars: A New Hope*, is released
1985 —	The computer game *Tetris* is created by Soviet Union engineer Alexey Pajitnov
1988 —	The Magellan Corporation's NAV 1000, the first handheld GPS device, goes on sale
1994 —	The underwater Channel Tunnel, or "Chunnel," opens, connecting Britain and France via the English Channel
2002 —	Halle Berry becomes the first Black actress to win the Best Actress Academy Award for her performance as Leticia Musgrove in the film *Monster's Ball*
2010 —	The Burj Khalifa skyscraper in Dubai opens, becoming the world's tallest building
2016 —	The Summer Olympics take place in Brazil, the first time the Olympic Games are played in South America
2022 —	The world passes the eight billion population mark

Bibliography

Dower, John, dir. *The Mystery of D.B. Cooper*. HBO, 2020.

FBI Records: The Vault: *D. B. Cooper*. https://vault.fbi.gov/D-B-Cooper%20.

Gray, Geoffrey. *Skyjack: The Hunt for D. B. Cooper*. New York: Crown Publishing Group, 2011.

"In Search of D.B. Cooper: Updates in the Unsolved Case," *FBI Archives*. March 17, 2009. https://archives.fbi.gov/archives/news/stories/2009/march/in-search-of-d.b.-cooper.

Koerner, Brendan. *The Skies Belong to Us: Love and Terror in the Golden Age of Hijacking*. New York: Crown Publishing Group, 2013.

"Money Analysis," *Citizen Sleuths*. https://citizensleuths.com/moneyanalysis.html.

Smith, Bruce A. "DB Cooper: An Interview with Former Case Agent Larry Carr," *The Mountain News—WA*. July 23, 2022. https://themountainnewswa.net/2022/07/23/db-cooper-an-interview-with-former-case-agent-larry-carr/.

Smith, Bruce A. "New Developments in the DB Cooper Case: Primary Witness Bill Mitchell Speaks Publicly for the First Time," *The Mountain News—WA*. December 7, 2014. https://themountainnewswa.net/2014/12/07/new-developments-in-the-db-cooper-case-primary-witness-bill-mitchell-speaks-publicaly/.

Stadiem, William. *Jet Set: The People, the Planes, the Glamour, and the Romance in Aviation's Golden Years*. New York: Ballantine Books, 2014.

"Titanium Particles from Cooper's Tie," *Citizen Sleuths*. https://citizensleuths.com/titaniumparticles.html.

Zenovich, Marina, dir. *D. B. Cooper: Where Are You?!* Netflix, 2022.